Fed fit

RECIPES FROM A CORNISH KITCHEN

Hettie Merrick

Tor Mark Press • Redruth

Cornish food is economical, plain and wholesome, with a few special treats. No matter that modern diets are low in carbohydrates – yeast and saffron cake, pasties, splits, 'heavy' cake and cream are as well loved as ever.

'It's a food that'd stick by 'ee,' is a remark often heard. Cornish mothers heave a sigh of relief when their sons marry local girls. They know 'they'll be fed fitty' and at least be sure of the weekly pasty.

The recipes I've gathered together for this book form the background to the main traditional meals – breakfast, dinner, tea and supper – that were eaten by most families during my childhood at Porthleven in West Cornwall. Many have been handed down to me by members of my own family. Others are from people who have become well known locally for their own particular speciality.

Most of the recipes are in metric, given that nearly everything we buy these days seems to have done away with imperial measurements. The exceptions are recipes taken from a booklet printed in 1939. For these, I've kept the old style, but have also given metric approximations.

I hope many people will be tempted to make their own pasties and try some of the enduring Cornish favourites.

THE TOR MARK SERIES

FOLKLORE

Classic Cornish ghost stories
Classic Devon ghost stories
Classic ghost stories from the
 Land's End
Classic West Country ghost stories
Cornish fairies
Cornish folklore

Cornish legends
Customs and superstitions
Demons, ghosts and spectres
Devon customs
Devon legends
Folk tales from the Land's End
The pixy book

OTHER TITLES

Charlestown
China clay
Classic Cornish anecdotes
Cornish fishing industry
Cornish mining – at surface
Cornish mining – underground
Cornish mining industry
Cornish recipes
Cornish saints
Cornish smuggling industry
Cornwall in camera
Cornwall's engine houses
Cornwall's railways
Devonshire jokes and stories
Do you know Cornwall?
Down 'long weth we
Exploring Cornwall with your car
Fed fitty
Jan Bedella's fiddle
Houses, castles and gardens
Introducing Cornwall
King Arthur – man or myth?

Lost ports of Cornwall
Old Cornwall – in pictures
The pasty book
Shipwrecks around Land's End
Shipwrecks around the Lizard
Shipwrecks around Mount's Bay
Shipwrecks – Falmouth to Looe
Shipwrecks – St Ives to Bude
Short Cornish dictionary
The story of Cornwall
The story of the Cornish language
The story of St Ives
The story of Truro Cathedral
Strange tales of the Cornish coast
Tales of the Cornish fishermen
Tales of the Cornish miners
Tales of the Cornish smugglers
Tales of the Cornish wreckers
Twelve walks on the Lizard
What shall we do with the smuggled
 brandy?

First published 1998 by Tor Mark Press
United Downs Industrial Estate, St Day, Redruth, Cornwall, TR16 5HY
© Tor Mark Press 1998
ISBN 0 85025-364-0
The illustrations and cover are by Amanda Wood
Printed in Great Britain by Burstwick Print and Publicity Services, Hull

BREAKFAST

The start of the day was usually a rush, but at home we managed porridge or shredded wheat followed by bread, toasted through the bars of the Cornish range on the prongs of a long wire toasting fork. Mother bought Dundee marmalade, sold in white, shiny pots. My grandparents on both sides considered all this new-fangled. They ate bread, butter and treacle or jam, or saffron buns with cocoa.

Food, though, has never tasted so good as it did at Content, an isolated farm cottage (now swallowed up by RNAS Culdrose) where I spent many of my childhood holidays with Aunt Hettie and Uncle Fred. First thing every morning eggs were fetched from a long row of chicken houses. I was allowed to carry my own egg for breakfast, warm and smooth in my hand. One old fowl was a household pet. She was lame and no one had the heart to kill her, so I had 'Miss Clutterbut's egg' for breakfast, or so I was told.

My aunt made bread once a week, putting the loaves into round cake tins to bake. To cut slices, she would hold the loaf crooked in her left arm resting against her pinny, and cut the bread towards herself with a worn but razor-sharp knife. As the week went by, the bread got drier and the slices thinner, till by bake day the slices were like wafers.

The bread was eaten to the last crust and rarely thrown out for the chickens. They got a good mix of vegetable peelings boiled up outside in an iron pot on a triangular brandis over a good fire.

Bread (and yeast cooking)

Plain flour must always be used for yeast cookery and strong flour gives the best results. Fresh yeast is easily obtainable in Cornwall, but dried yeast is almost as good. Some people cream yeast with a little sugar but when making bread this can sweeten it; my family prefers the yeast whisked in a little water or milk. The main thing is to keep the yeast dough out of any draughts. A sunny spot is good, but room heat is sufficient now that cold kitchens are a thing of the past.

Fifty years ago the bowls of dough were put to rise in the rack of the Cornish range – 'the slab'. My aunts sponged their yeast by making a hole in the flour, pouring the yeast in with a little milk, and sprinkling some flour over to cover. The bowl would be covered with a damp cloth and put in the rack. Every now and then the corner of the cloth would be lifted and they would peep inside to see if the yeast had bubbled through. When it had, they lifted down the bowl, mixed the cake, pummelled the dough and put it back again to prove, or 'to plumb', as we say.

It all takes time. There is an expression still often used when someone does something they might regret: 'She'll wish her cake dough,' said with a shake of the head, 'she'll wish her cake dough.'

Bread recipe

Note: The quantities are for more than one loaf, as it is a waste of oven space to bake just one. Bread freezes well.

1.5kg strong white flour	25g yeast
50g lard	3 teaspoons salt

900ml tepid water (or three quarters water, one quarter milk)
Whisk the yeast into half a pint of the liquid. Put the flour and salt in a bowl and rub in the fat. Pour in the yeast and the remaining liquid. Mix and knead well till the mixture leaves the bowl clean. Cover with a cloth or put into a lightly greased polythene bag to prove. When the dough has doubled in size, knead it again and mould into loaves. Put into well-greased tins to just below the top. Prove again till the bread is just above the tin. Put in a hot oven (around 425°F, 220°C, gas mark 7) and bake for one hour. Turn out of the tin at once, onto a cooling rack.

Bread sops (Gran's between meals filler)

Cut a thick piece of bread from a loaf, break it up into small pieces and place in a cup. Pour on boiling water and drain it off again, squeezing the bread with the back of a spoon till the bread is dry and crumbly. Season with salt and pepper, place a large piece of butter on top and eat at once with a teaspoon. It is impossible to make this with modern sliced bread: home made bread or bread that will crumb is the only kind suitable. It was sometimes made with cocoa.

DINNER TIME

After breakfast at Content, water was fetched from the spring below the henhouse. The water gushed out freezing cold from a pipe into a granite trough, spilling out and running down the valley. Water was carried in large brown earthenware pitchers, but first we filled up the split bicycle tyres for the chickens to drink from.

When it was time to cook dinner (which was usually eaten at noon), we went up to the garden to get the vegetables, and to pick fruit for tarts for afters, or for tea.

Beef and pork were eaten for the main daily meals; though my mother often cooked lamb with mint or caper sauce, I cannot remember Gran cooking it. Gran liked a piece of beef with a bit of fat. She bought a little frying steak surprisingly often, and streaky pork for the under-roast.

Rabbit in season was very popular. We got it from Content, where Uncle Fred used snares (thankfully banned now) or it had been shot in the harvest field fleeing from the last standing corn. Some men went 'lamping' with dogs or used ferrets to chase rabbits from their holes. The downs nearby were a network of warrens.

Beyond the Downs, Gran and Grandad Bray lived at Gunwalloe. They lived well: there was a daily bowl of cream from Sam, Grandad's brother next door, who kept two Jersey cows. Gran also made cream from the milk she fetched in a large jug twice a day from her neighbour's farm. There was so much cream that Gran – 'Mother Matt' as everyone in the village called her – made all her own butter. Grandad kept pigs and chickens, so they had plenty of eggs and pork. Vegetables and corn for the chickens came from the farms in exchange for an odd day's work by Grandad. Apples and medlars came from Hingey orchard, gooseberries and rhubarb from the garden. Grandad was very fond of honey: this he had to buy! It was wartime and every

Saturday Gran came over to us with a basket full of eggs, butter, cream, and a fruit or seed cake.

Grandad Bray ate only under-roast potatoes with his meat and vegetables. I never saw him eat fish. Puddings were limited to a choice of three – junket, milk puddings, or fruit tart, always with lashings of cream and accompanied by a single cracker biscuit. The tarts, when cooked and sugared were carefully put onto a second plate to protect the cloth from juice; they waited on the table, the wafer-thin top floating on a sea of warm juicy fruit. At Content, Uncle Fred had a dinner-plate-sized tart for himself. Aunt Hettie's would be a medium plate and mine a large tea-plate. I felt it was like the three bears sitting at table.

One day, Thelma my eldest cousin brought her fiancé Charles over to Content for the day. He was considered a bit posh. He worked at 'The Mount' as under butler for Lord St Levan. When his tart was put in front of him he was very puzzled. I don't know if he managed to eat most of it, but Aunt Hettie always chuckled as she remembered his face when he realised he was expected to eat it all.

In winter broth was made often, simmering on the top of the range all morning. Sometimes large white beans, which had been soaked, were added.

But for many people, of course, dinner in Cornwall is the famous pasty:

Matthew, Mark, Luke and John
Ate a pasty five foot long.
Ate it once, ate it twice,
Oh my Lor', it's full of mice.

All Cornish children learn this ditty and have their own pasty from toddler days, and any visitor to a Cornish town at noon cannot fail to notice a cross-section of people, smart office men and women, hefty workmen, youngsters and mums pushing prams, eating their lunch as they go along, 'a pasty in their hand,' as a local song puts it. So the traditional pasty must be the first item in this section of my Cornish recipe book.

Pasty pastry

500g strong white flour (pinch of salt optional)
125g margarine (Echo)   125g lard   200ml water to mix

Put the margarine in the freezer for ten minutes. Place the flour in a bowl and rub in the lard. Grate the margarine and stir into the flour with a knife. Pour in cold water. Mix with a knife till absorbed. Knead the mixture a little and leave it at least half an hour before using – or make it the day before and store in the fridge overnight.

Filling for one Cornish pasty

50g finely sliced swede (always referred to as 'turnip')
25g finely sliced onion   75-100g beef (skirt or chuck)
175g sliced old potatoes   salt and pepper

Keep the sliced potatoes in a basin of cold water till needed. Trim off any gristle and cut the meat into 6mm (¹/₄ inch) pieces including some fat. Cut off 100g of made pastry and shape it roughly like a ball. Roll out into a large round the size of a dinner plate.

Place the onion along the centre of the pastry and cover with a layer of turnip. Sprinkle well with pepper and a shake of salt. Place the meat along the top and to the ends. (The 'ends' are the corners and the cook must make sure that the meat is spread into the corners.) Season the meat with salt. Top this layer with most of the potato, salt lightly and place the remainder of the potato on top. Seasoning is important to the taste of a pasty and only experience can perfect it.

Moisten the further half of the edge of the circle with water and fold it over to seal. Press the sides of pastry together, from the middle outwards towards each 'end', pressing gently and firmly. 'Crimp' the edge from right to left by folding the pastry edge over and over in a rope pattern, tucking in the end when you reach the other side. Place the pasties apart on a flat baking tray. Brush with beaten egg or milk.

Some people put a knob of butter in the pasty: I don't think this is necessary, but it may be traditional. There was often very little beef available and in that case the butter would help make gravy.

Pasties are 'pressure cooked'. I don't make a hole in mine to let the steam out, though some people do. Place in a hot oven (425°F, 220°C, gas mark 7) on a shelf three quarters of the way up from the bottom and 'bake like fate' for 15-20 minutes.

Check the pasties; if nicely brown, place them on a lower shelf and turn the oven down to 350°F (180°C, gas mark 4) and cook for a further 25 minutes, then turn the oven off altogether. Keep the oven door shut and leave for a further 10 minutes. Remove from the oven and let them rest for a few minutes before serving.

[Many pasty variations can be found in *The Pasty Book*, by the same author in the Tor Mark paperback series.]

Mock flaky pastry (for sausage rolls, etc)

Roll out 450g made-up pastry into an oblong. Dab 125g butter on two thirds of the area. Fold over the unbuttered side and fold over again. Rest the pastry for 30 minutes. Roll out and fold in three again. Rest a little before use. (If you freeze the pastry at this stage, defrost, roll out, and fold in three again. Rest 15 minutes before using.)

Broth, for 4 persons

450g flank or stewing beef, in one piece	
a quarter to a half cauliflower head	
3 large slices of swede	2 onions or shallots
half a leek, sliced thinly	2 or 3 carrots and a parsnip
salt and pepper	a bay leaf
a frond of parsley	1.75 litres water or cabbage stock

Fry the meat on all sides for a minute in a little butter. Add the water or stock, bring to the boil and simmer for one hour, skimming off any scum. Add the vegetables except the cauliflower, chopped into bite-sized pieces. Simmer for another 30 minutes. Add the cauliflower (cut into large pieces), the seasoning, bay leaf and parsley. Simmer till cooked. Remove bay leaf and parsley. Check the liquid level and remove the meat to a plate. Cut up the meat and return to the broth if you wish, or reserve it to eat with boiled potatoes. There should be nearly two litres of soup; add dumplings if liked.

Rabbit pie

Skin and clean the rabbit and wash again in salted water. Disjoint and place the rabbit pieces in a saucepan with a little carrot, onion and turnip, salt, pepper and a bay leaf. Cover with water, bring to the boil and simmer until tender. Place pieces of rabbit in a pie dish with pieces of turnip and carrot; remove the bay leaf. Pour some of the liquid into the dish. Cover with thick pastry, placing an upturned eggcup in the dish to keep the pastry up in the middle. Bake in a hot oven till the pastry is cooked.

Chicken or fowl pie can be made in the same way, and parsley can be added.

Beef and tatie pie, for 4 persons

450g stewing beef	1 large onion
half a small turnip	500g potatoes
pepper and salt	125g made up pastry
1 or 2 cups water (approx. 250 to 500 ml)	

Cut the beef into small chunks and fry a little, with a knob of butter, until brown on all sides. Place in a saucepan with one cup of water, onion and seasoning. Cover with a lid, bring to the boil and simmer for at least 30 minutes. Add the turnip and potatoes sliced up thickly and simmer till the vegetables are just cooked. (If the stew dries out, add water to make some gravy.) Season and pour all the contents into a deep pie dish. Cover with rolled out fairly thick pastry and immediately place in an oven at 450⁰F (230⁰C, gas mark 8) to cook for 15-20 minutes. Serve with cabbage or other vegetables.

Stew, for four persons

450g stewing steak	8 large potatoes
$1/4$ medium swede	4 or 5 carrots, and parsnip if liked
2 or 3 onions, shallots or leeks to taste	

Cut the meat into small chunks and fry in a large saucepan with a piece of butter (25g) until brown on all sides. Cover the meat with water. Bring to the boil, then simmer for 45 minutes. Add the chopped prepared vegetables and pepper and salt. My aunt used to say, 'give it a good gallop,' but simmering is what is required, stirring it around occasionally and adjusting the liquid with water.

Dumplings can be added ten minutes before dishing up.

Dumplings

Mix 50g shredded suet to 100g self-raising flour and a good pinch of salt. Add about 75 ml water to make a soft dough. Divide into eight shapes and poach on top of the stew for ten minutes.

Many years ago, my sister-in-law when newly married made my brother stew once a week. One day he hinted he wouldn't mind a dumpling or two. Sylvia asked my mother for instructions. Mother said, 'you double the amount of flour to suet and simply mix it all with water. Sylvia did this, using the whole packet of suet. The lid of the saucepan rose higher and higher, and when they came to eating the stew had disappeared entirely; but love prevailed and my brother ate most of it.

Leeky pie (Mrs Sylvia Oliver, Goon Rinsey)

Cut 500g chuck or braising steak into cubes and season with a little salt. Barely cover with water and casserole it till tender. Meanwhile, partly cook some leeks, then cut them up and layer them on top of the meat. Spread cream over if you have it handy (you can tell this recipe came from a farm!) or butter and pepper well, cover with flaky or pasty pastry and bake till brown.

VEGETABLES

Fishermen have no time to dig a garden. When in from the sea there is work to be done, nets mended, and the boat seen to. Their houses, anyway, were built either perched on the edge of the cliff or sheltering underneath, close to the road, with little ground either front or back. There might just have been enough room to grow a bay tree for the pilchards, or a bush of boy's love, useful to keep the flies away. Potatoes and turnip, bolstered with carrot, leek, onion, parsnip and broccoli (cauliflower) grown by the farmer were the vegetables eaten, helped out with dried peas and lentils.

My father never tasted a tomato till he got married and never got to like them. Celery, lettuce or cress he considered rabbit food. Mother was in her element cooking. She would cook strange things at home, like mushrooms or artichokes, and made delicious sauces: father couldn't abide sauces and, like most Cornishmen, he hated food 'mucked up'.

Potatoes were served very plainly: boiled with fish, under-roast every other meal, chips or raw tatie fry for tea. Under-roast was the easiest. The slab was always lit and potatoes in the oven left the top clear for a kettle on the boil, the iron, cooking vegetables or the large oval iron pot for washing clothes.

Under-roast potatoes

Bring peeled potatoes to the boil, cook a little and drain. Grease a pie dish with butter or dripping and fill with potatoes. Add a couple of small onions and a few pieces of turnip if liked. Season the potatoes with salt and a good shake of pepper. Brush some dripping over the potatoes or cover with a few bacon rinds, and half fill the dish with hot water. Place another dish over the top as a lid, or cover with greaseproof paper. Put in a hot oven for a good half-hour. Take off the paper and cook for another hour or so until the tops of the potatoes are nice and brown and the water almost gone. The result should be crispy brown topped potatoes with mushy bottoms. Sometimes a piece of meat would be cooked in the middle and always Granny Gilbert baked a roll of pastry across the top.

Raw tatie fry

Fry two rashers of streaky or other bacon in a frying pan. Add sliced raw peeled potatoes till the pan is nearly full, sprinkle with some salt and pepper and pour in water until the potato is almost covered. Cover pan, bring to the boil and cook gently for about an hour. (Some people add onion.) The water should be absorbed, but not dried out.

Gran Gilbert, who lived at the bottom of the steps linking the Terrace with the centre of the village, 'up long' with 'down long', was the pivot round which all her grandchildren gathered. She could always produce something for us to eat and often warmed us up on winter evenings with raw tatie fry, bread or cocoa sops (see page 5) or a cup of broth (see page 8).

Potato cake – method 1

225g plain flour	50g lard
75g suet or margarine	225g fresh mashed potatoes
1 level teaspoon salt	

Mix together. Roll out onto a floured board and cut into rounds. Bake at 400ºF (200ºC, gas mark 6) till brown and crisp.

Potato cake – method 2

Mix together 450g mashed potatoes, 100g sultanas, two tablespoons each self-raising and plain flour, 50g suet and some salt and pepper to taste. Shape into rounds and bake till brown and crisp.

Mashed turnip

Prepare a swede (always referred to as 'turnip' in Cornwall) and cut into pieces. Put into a saucepan and cover with cold water. Add some salt, bring to the boil, and cook till tender. Drain off the water. Season with a good shake of pepper and a little ground nutmeg, and add more salt if need be. Keep hot and, just before dishing up, mash well with a good tablespoon of thick cream or butter.

This was Mother Matt's recipe. I remember watching the colour of the mashed turnip change dramatically when the cream was added. It tastes wonderful but I can never bring myself to be so extravagant.

AFTERS

Britain is famous for its puddings and the Cornish share a great love of 'afters', most of which can be served with cream. We ate jam roly-poly, egg custard, tarts made with blackberry, blackcurrant, gooseberry, apple, rhubarb or plum; also prunes and custard or prunes still warm with cream – delicious. Rice, sago and tapioca were often made as well, and Mother always made treacle pudding on Sundays. Jellies, blancmange and Russian cream were usually reserved for Sunday, along with trifle.

Cream (home made)

Pour at least four pints of fresh milk into a large saucepan. Let it rest all morning and carefully place the saucepan on the stove. Bring it slowly to a temperature just below boiling; it must not begin to rise. Gently put it to one side and leave overnight in a cool place Next morning skim off the top into a dish. Use the remaining 'scalded' milk for puddings or milky drinks.

Real Cornish cream is made by scalding separated milk until a delicious thick crust is formed.

Bread pudding

Crusts or half a stale loaf soaked in a litre of water
a couple of handfuls of currants and sultanas
stale cake or buns, if you have them, crumbled
grated rind and the juice of half a lemon

a little mixed peel	a pinch of salt
2 tablespoons sugar	a few chopped dates
125g margarine	2 tablespoons syrup
1 or 2 eggs	1 teaspoon bicarbonate of soda
1-2 teaspoons mixed spice	

Squeeze the water out of the bread and place the bread in a bowl. Add all the other ingredients except the margarine, syrup, lemon juice and bicarbonate of soda. Melt the margarine and syrup in a pan and add to the mixture. Mix the bicarbonate of soda with lemon juice and stir in immediately; mix all together. Smooth out into a large greased baking dish and fork a pattern on top. Cook in a slow to moderate oven: around 325-350ºF (170-180ºC, gas mark 3-4) for about an hour or more. Sprinkle with a little sugar and eat either hot or cold.

Apple tart

Pile an old dinner plate or pie dish with as much peeled and sliced cooking apple as it can hold. Moisten with a tablespoon of water. Cover the apple with pastry, rolled out quite thinly, making sure you don't pull the pastry tightly, so that it can shrink a bit.

Bake in a hot oven till cooked. Remove from the oven and carefully lift off the pastry top (slice around the edge with a knife before lifting). Sugar the contents and when the apple has cooled a bit replace the lid.

Serve slightly warm with plenty of cream.

Shortcrust pastry is not suitable for this tart. Pasty pastry holds together better.

Cooked apple

We ate apple all ways. Simply stewed and eaten with custard, or stewed with suet dumplings over; large apples cored and filled with brown sugar, baked and brought out of the oven at just the moment when the fluffy apples were lifting the scored skin around their sides and the juice like toffee in the tray; baked with a coat of pastry they looked even bigger. There were tarts of course, and apples cooked with a topping of sponge or baked in the oven sliced between thin slices of bread and butter, cinnamon and sugar.

Autumn was a feast in those days. Most of us knew or had someone in the family working on a farm and were given a bag or two full of windfalls. Nowadays orchards and fields are being cleared to make way for housing or larger fields and those wonderful old-fashioned apples are disappearing, some gone for ever.

Junket

Warm one pint of milk to blood heat with 2 dessertspoons sugar. Pour 2 teaspoons rennet into a large jug and add the warmed milk and sugar. Pour out at once into two or three dishes, which you should have placed where they need not be moved till dinner time. Do not put in the fridge. When needed, sprinkle with nutmeg to taste, and serve with at least 25g cream per person. Junket can be made an hour or more in advance.

Rice pudding with egg

Make rice pudding in the usual way. Ten minutes before dishing up, add one beaten egg to the pudding, stirring it in carefully so that the skin is not disturbed. Sprinkle the pudding lightly with nutmeg.

This was a favourite with Granny Gilbert, who made wonderful rice puddings. She could not afford cream, but nursed the pudding along all morning on the bottom shelf of the oven, adding extra milk now and then. She would often add an egg for 'extra goodness'.

Cornish Christmas pudding

6 eggs	450g shredded suet
900g raisins	450g currants
450g sultanas	225g peel
350g sugar	350g self-raising flour
50g chopped almonds	a good pinch of salt
1 grated lemon rind and juice	450g breadcrumbs
half a nutmeg, grated	1 level teaspoon spice
300 ml brandy	

Mix all together. Put into basins. Cover with greaseproof paper. Tie down and steam for seven hours.

Russian cream

2 eggs	600 ml milk
25g gelatine	50g sugar

Add gelatine to enough hot water to melt it. Separate the egg yolks from the whites into two separate bowls and beat the yolks with the sugar. Put the milk on to boil and when the milk begins to rise in the pan pour in the beaten egg yolks and sugar. Remove from the heat. Stir in the gelatine. Beat the egg whites till stiff enough to turn the bowl upside down without them slipping out! Pour the egg yolk mixture onto the egg whites and then pour it all into a serving dish.

Put in a cool place to set. Russian cream is usually made the day before you need it, and served with seedless grapes.

I am always puzzled by where this much loved delicate sweet came from, as it is so different from all other Cornish cooking.

THE GUNWALLOE RECIPES

To my surprise one day, Mrs Dale, a farmer's wife, asked me if I had ever seen a booklet printed in 1939, written by members of the Methodist Chapel at Gunwalloe; it's a little treasure, full of worthy advice, sayings and – best of all – their favourite recipes which follow. Because of the recipes' age, all the ingredients are in imperial quantities, but I've also provided rough metric equivalents for those who prefer to keep to grams and litres.

Toffee pudding for children
(Mrs Hocking, Truro)

$1/2$ lb (225g) treacle [syrup] $1/4$ lb (115g) butter
$1/4$ lb (115g) brown sugar   3 slices bread $1/2$ in (1.25cm thick)

Place the treacle, butter and sugar in a frying pan and stir till melted. Remove crusts from bread and cut into two inch squares. Soak these in milk and fry them in the toffee for about 5 minutes. Place in a hot dish, pour on the remaining toffee and serve.

Fig pudding
(Mrs Delora Jenkin, Nanspean Farm, Gunwalloe)

4oz (115g) shredded suet   4oz (115g) flour
4oz (115g) breadcrumbs   4oz (115g) brown sugar
$3/4$ lb (340g) figs [or dates]   1 large apple
1 teaspoon baking powder $1/4$ pint (150ml) milk

Chop the figs and apple fine, mix flour and baking powder well, add dry ingredients with milk to moisten them. Pour into greased basin and steam for $2^1/2$ hours. (Sufficient for 8-10 persons.)

Banana pudding
(Mrs H C Lugg, Post Office, Gunwalloe)

$1/2$ lb (225g) self-raising flour $1/4$ lb (115g) butter
$1/4$ lb (115g) castor sugar   4 bananas
2 eggs

Beat all together before adding flour. Bake about $1^1/2$ hours.

'Helston pudding'
(Miss Margaret Freeman, Tregadjack, Mawgan)

4 oz (115g) raisins	4 oz (115g) currants
4 oz (115g) flour	4 oz (115g) ground rice
4 oz (115g) sugar	small piece of peel
4 oz (115g) breadcrumbs	6 oz (175g) suet
1 teaspoon mixed spice	a little salt
some milk	1 teaspoon bicarbonate of soda

Clean the fruit, cut the peel finely, and dissolve the bicarbonate of soda in the milk. Mix together all the dry ingredients and add the milk. When thoroughly mixed, pour into a well greased basin, cover with greased paper and a floured pudding cloth tied securely. Stand in a saucepanful of boiling water and boil for two hours.

TEA

Everyday teatime in our family was a brief meal. A cup of tea and a bun or perhaps a piece of bread, butter and treacle.

I often went to Aunt Violet's for tea. She had a large family and I squeezed in beside my cousins on the wooden form around the table, drinking strong dark cocoa and eating coconut haystacks or a piece of 'jam paste' – which I liked so much it became their nickname for me.

Sometimes Uncle George would make his speciality, potato fritters. What a wonderful way to fill up a growing family. A few potatoes would be sliced very finely, dipped into fresh batter and dropped into hot fat in the frying pan. They were usually cooked in the scullery beside the kitchen and brought to us in relays. We could hear them sizzling, and then they would come in, all hot, crisp and salty.

Gran sat on a hard chair at the back of the room, her hands resting on the crook of her walking stick. Aunt Violet sat by the slab with a short cane handy by to keep order. Her two eldest boys often got a crack. They were two 'lembs' (limbs of the devil). Tucked away in the corner there always seemed to be a new baby which Aunt Violet rocked and sang off to sleep in a sweet, soft voice.

All the bakers sold good bread. Mother bought most of her bread from Johns', one of whose sons brought bread around in a large wicker basket to the customers' houses. He often sat down for a short spell, resting his arms at the end of the table, probably while Mother was hunting for her purse. His transport was a pony and a neat little van. The milkmen too delivered milk from their ponies and traps, carrying large cans of milk, and measured out the pints into jugs at the doorstep.

With good fresh bread, there is nothing to beat a slice of 'thunder and lightning'. Cut a thick slice of fresh bread and spread the surface well with syrup and then thickly with clotted cream. Some people dribble a trickle of syrup over the top to make a pattern. The cool cream, sweet syrup and crusty bread make a wonderful combination. Cornish people often make sandwiches with Turkish Delight, fruit cake, ginger biscuits, banana, jam, grated chocolate or Mars bars. Cream on splits, sprinkled with sugar, is also popular.

For special occasions, a few iced fancies, slab cake, Scribona swiss roll, or congress tarts would be bought.

Chapel teas

These are held with great enjoyment and follow a time-honoured pattern.

Long tables are made up of trestles and planks to go the whole length of the Sunday School. The tables are covered with starched white damask table-cloths and laid with bone china, plain white, bordered in silver or gold leaf with the Chapel's name proudly marked. Large plates laden with splits, buttered or spread with jam and cream, white and saffron cake, and slab (fruit cake) are put out together with vases of flowers here and there.

Old photographs of chapel teas show the tables laid out of doors with no cover. This tradition continues at Porthleven's St Peterstide Sunday School Treat, but now a large marquee is hired.

At both ends of each table, the young ladies pour the tea and wait on everyone, bringing the cups of tea down the table and making sure your cup is refilled as soon as it is empty. What a thrill it was to reach the age to be allowed to help. In the vestry, older ladies keep stocks up, the water boiling and prepare fresh platefuls of cake to replace the emptying ones.

Without ever being told, you knew that manners demanded you should start with a buttered split, and that though you could eat as much as you liked of the cake, it would be greedy to eat more than one 'fancy'. Tea would be as most Cornish like it, very hot and strong with little milk.

After tea, while the women washed up, the men dismantled the tables and games were played: Nursery Rhymes, Spinning the Plate,

Stations, Passing the Parcel. When we were young we would ask for Postman's Knock but the elders knew better and it was banned.

Faith tea

Faith tea is similar to Chapel Tea but food is not bought. Every family brings a plateful of something, and it is surprising that the right proportion of savouries and fancies turn up, seemingly with no consultation.

Jam paste (pasty pastry with jam)

Roll out the pastry into a round. Brush a little butter or margarine onto one half. Fold over and bake in a hot oven for 15 minutes or so. Split open when cooked. Spread with jam (and cream if liked).

Date pasty (mock flaky pastry)

Place the dates in a bowl. Pour on boiling water and drain immediately. Roll out the pastry into a round: spread the dates thickly onto one half. Fold over the other half of the roll lightly with the rolling pin. Egg wash and bake in a moderate to hot oven, about 375°F (190°C, gas mark 5). Slices of cooking apples may be added to the dates. Alternatively an Eccles cake mixture can be used – 25g butter, 50g brown sugar, 20g currants with a little peel, a dash of cinnamon.

Milk splits

450g strong white flour	25g yeast
50g lard	1/2 teaspoon salt
300ml milk, or milk and water	

Whisk the yeast into the tepid or cold liquid. Place the flour in a bowl, mix in the salt and rub in the fat. Pour in the liquid and knead well. Put in a lightly oiled polythene bag or cover the mixture with a cloth and leave to prove. When it's doubled in size, cut into about ten 'splits' by moulding the pieces into balls, placing them on a greased tray quite close together and flattening the top lightly with the hand. Prove again. When the splits have doubled in size again (after about 20 minutes) bake in a hot oven 400-425⁰F (200C-220⁰C, gas mark 6-7) for about 15 minutes. They are cooked when the bottoms are light brown. When cool, cut the splits in half sideways; spread each half with strawberry, blackberry or blackcurrant jam and put a large dollop of cream on top.

'Cornish cream teas' are a popular commercial treat, but scones (foreign and easier to make) have crept in instead of proper splits.

Yeast cake

(Mrs June Hosking, Chyvarloe Farm, Gunwalloe)

1.5 kg strong flour (and a pinch of salt)	
450g fruit (sultanas and, if you like, about 25g peel)	
40g yeast	225g Trex
275g margarine	175g sugar
3 eggs	approx. 560 ml of milk to mix

Whisk the yeast into a little milk. Place the flour and salt in a bowl. Rub the fats into the flour; add sugar and fruit. Pour in the yeast liquid, the eggs and the remainder of the milk and stir with a knife to mix, then knead well. Cover the dough with a cloth and leave to prove. When it's doubled in size, knead again. Divide and mould into cakes, putting the dough into well greased tins. When it has risen again, place the cakes in an oven at 300⁰F (150⁰C, gas mark 2) and bake for one hour. Turn the cakes out onto a wire tray.

This very good recipe can also be adapted for saffron (see below).

Note: when using an electric mixer for yeast cakes, make the dough up and knead well before adding the fruit by hand. Fruit, especially currants, can discolour the dough when mixed in a machine.

Yeast buns

450g strong white flour and a pinch of salt
50g margarine (or butter)   50g sugar
50g lard   175g sultanas
a little peel (optional)   25g yeast
1 egg (optional)
1 large cup milk (about 250 ml) to mix

This recipe makes 16 – 20 buns. Whisk the yeast into tepid or cold milk. Warm the flour if possible (not vital) and add the salt. Rub in the fats. Add the sugar and fruit, and mix in. Pour in the liquid and mix with a knife till all the liquid is absorbed. Finish by hand and knead well. Put the dough in a greased polythene bag or leave in a bowl and cover with a cloth to prove. When it has doubled in size, knead again lightly. Divide into 16 to 20 buns and place on a lightly greased baking tray. When the buns have doubled again, bake in the oven at 400ºF (200ºC, gas mark 6) for about 15 minutes. They are cooked when brown on the bottom.

Bun dough should be of a softer consistency than cake mixture.

When I was a little 'maid' I was often puzzled by the expression, he or she's 'as soft as Bunda'. Who was Bunda? I thought it must be a nickname; most men in fishing villages are known only by a nickname. I was grown up before I realised that 'Bunda' was bun dough.

Saffron

Saffron is the stamens of a certain type of crocus and nowadays it is imported mostly from Spain, although it is said that until the eighteenth century it was grown at Saffron Walden in Essex. Weight for weight it is more expensive than gold. 'As dear as saffron' is a very common Cornish expression. When I was sent sixty years ago for a shilling's worth, the grocer weighed a measure on special scales. In those days that amount of saffron coloured and flavoured 1.5kg of flour to a glorious yellow. Ten grains of saffron now costs nearly £2 and scarcely colours the same quantity darker than a primrose.

Saffron should be prepared the day before you need it. Place the strands in a cup. Pour boiling water on, and quarter fill the cup. Cover and leave in a safe place till use.

I lived in Stithians for a while and my neighbour, an elderly lady, Mrs Bath, prepared her saffron in a different way from any I had seen. She put her saffron between greaseproof paper and very carefully dried the strands. Then she rolled her rolling pin over the paper: this reduced the contents to powder. She said she got more flavour and colour from her saffron. I tried it once or twice, but I scorched the saffron and it was ruined, so I stick to soaking the strands, which I prefer to see in cakes.

Saffron buns

450g strong white flour and a pinch of salt

225g cleaned currants	25g sultanas
50g sugar	50g butter
50g lard	25g fresh yeast or equivalent dried
250 ml (approx.) milk to mix	peel, to taste

10 grains saffron (prepared the night before)

Whisk the yeast into the milk. Place the flour in a bowl with the salt and rub in the fats. Add the sugar and fruit, and stir in. Pour in the saffron first and rinse out the cup with the milk and yeast liquid. Mix the ingredients with a knife and then knead well. Put the dough aside in a bowl covered with a cloth to prove. When the dough has doubled in size, knead and divide into about 20 buns by shaping into balls and placing them on a greased baking tray. Flatten the tops of the buns with the hand and leave to prove again (about 20 minutes), covering with a cloth. When the dough has doubled in size, bake at 400°F (200°C, gas mark 6) for about 15-20 minutes. They are cooked when brown on the bottom. An egg can be added to this recipe, adjusting the liquid if necessary.

Saffron cake
(Mrs Lilian Stephens, Helston)

1kg strong white flour	175g butter
275g sugar	40g yeast
200g lard	325g currants
100g sultanas	25g peel
1 egg (optional)	1 packet saffron (10 grains)
400 ml milk and water	

Steep the saffron overnight. Put the yeast into a teaspoonful of sugar and stir. Put the flour and salt in a bowl; rub in the fats. Add the sugar and stir in the fruit. Pour in the saffron and rinse out the cup with the milk; add the yeast liquid. Break the egg into the mixture, and mix with a knife till all the moisture is absorbed. Knead well. Cover the bowl with a cloth or put it in a polythene bag to prove. When it has doubled in size, knead lightly again. Cut the dough and place into well greased tins, three quarter filling them. Prove again. When the dough has risen a little way over the top of the tin, bake at 325⁰F (170⁰C, gas mark 3) for about an hour. When cooked, turn out at once onto a wire tray.

Not long ago I was reminiscing with Uncle Charlie. As children, his daughter and I were sent down to the quay with his 'croust' – a pint of hot strong tea in an enamel can with a cup hooked on the top and a couple of pieces of cake. It was almost always saffron cake and I commented to him that it was an expensive cake to be made so often, and for croust! 'Well, my dear,' he said, 'I was earning really good money at that time, £7 or £8 a week.'

It certainly was, but he earned it. His eyes used to be two rounds in a black face except where sweat ran down in trickles. He worked on the coal boats, helping unload tons of coal into the yards nearby. Everywhere along the harbour was covered in thick black coal dust.

Aunt Hartie, his wife, made a good saffron cake. She did something Mother never did: she would cut across the dough with a big cross before proving. As the dough 'plumbed', the cross would get larger and larger. It served no purpose, but I have heard since that many housewives do this, probably unaware of the origin, making a sign of the cross to keep evil away. Mother only cut a cross on her Easter Friday saffron buns, made in place of hot cross buns.

One Christmas, Aunt Violet's saffron cake was a disaster. It didn't rise and the cake was heavy. There was a great discussion and some concern about this. In the end it was agreed among the aunts and mother that it was too rich, too much goodness. I can remember visiting the house with Gran the day the cake was made and Aunt Violet taking down the bowl from the rack of the slab and anxiously examining the golden mound that was refusing to budge. Looking back, I don't think it was 'too much goodness' that did the damage. Aunt Violet liked a good fire. The grate doors were often open, showing bright red embers through the iron bars. A wisp of steam always curled from a large black kettle on the range. When you had a cup of tea or cocoa you had to sip carefully lest you burnt your lip; the whole room was warm and cosy. I think the yeast was overcome by heat and expired. It's better to put a yeast mixture in the fridge overnight than near heat, though I do put the second proving near gentle warmth or on a sunny window ledge, so long as it's clear of any draught.

FEAST DAYS

Large saffron buns are the 'feast' bun of Cornwall. The bun, shrunk now from 30cm to 15cm (12 in to 6 in) in diameter, is called a 'Tea Treat Bun'. Porthleven's feast day is 29 June, St Peter's Day or St Peterstide, and the Feast is now held on the Saturday nearest this date, the Chapel joining with the Anglican church to make it a special day. The members set off from one of the places of worship at 2.30 pm to walk about three miles around the 'town', led by the band and the churches' banners, to the recreation field, where every child of the Sunday schools is handed their bun. Gallons of scalding free tea is ready for anyone, prepared in the football team's changing hut.

The thrill of this day was greater than any other holiday, more important than Christmas, Easter or birthdays. Relations from near and far came 'home' for the day and bunting hung from window to window outside the houses. White socks, plimsolls and new clothes had been waiting for weeks to be worn and the weather was discussed endlessly. Would it keep up if good, or clear if poor?

The atmosphere in the Sunday school, where for the last month we had been reluctantly drilled and taught our lines for Anniversary under the eagle eye of 'Popsie', was electric. By the time the procession set off, we were nearly worn out with excitement and running round – up one set of stairs, tip-toeing across the gallery, and down the other. The men, busy unfurling the large flags and beautiful blue and gold banner, for once turned a blind eye to our unholy behaviour. Outside, the bandsmen would be gathering, smart in their uniforms, chatting and smoking a last cigarette before the long walk.

All Cornish villages have their Feast Day, but only a few now march through the streets. The 'days', a whisper of our Celtic past, stretch all through the year according to whichever saint is remembered. It meant a day off from school, and was a nuisance for the County Education Office.

St Keverne Feast bun
(Mrs Mavis Sobey)

10 grains saffron prepared overnight
225g plain flour and a pinch of salt

225g self-raising flour	200g castor sugar
250g butter	175g dried fruit
milk and water to mix	egg and syrup for glaze

Rub the fat into the flour and salt. Add the dry ingredients and mix with the saffron and milk to form a dough that's a little softer than a pastry mixture. Roll out a little thinner than for scones. Glaze with a mixture of egg and syrup. Mark a cross on the top with the back of a knife. Bake at 400°F (200°C, gas mark 6) for 15-20 minutes.

I was given this recipe by Mrs Mavis Sobey and would be interested to know if it is made in any other area. It is new to me and interesting, as it is a sort of saffroned 'heavy cake'. Mrs Sobey reduces the saffron to powder when she makes these buns.

Seed cake

This cake was made very often by my mother and Gran Bray. It is about the only thing I cannot eat: I'd sooner eat snails. My mother would make up her yeast cake mix without the fruit and divide a piece off for her 'seedy cake', adding about two tablespoons to a 2lb (1kg) tin. Granny Bray, who never cooked with yeast, made a cake with a rubbing in method, which would have been 225g self raising flour, 85-115g butter, 85-115g sugar, 1 egg and a good tablespoon of caraway seeds mixed with milk or sour cream to a little softer consistency than rock buns. Put into an 8 inch (20cm) cake tin and bake at 350ºF (180ºC, gas mark 4) for about an hour.

Heavy cake

Heavy cake was, and is, a good standby. It is eggless and easily made. Farmers' wives made 'sheaves' full to be taken out in flaskets for croust in the fields at harvest time. Fresh and hot, with welcome cups of tea, it is surprisingly delicious. There are a great many recipes for heavy cake: here are two.

Heavy cake made up light

450g self-raising flour	100g lard
125g butter or margarine	100g sugar
300ml milk to mix	1 egg (optional)
a little peel (optional)	a good pinch of salt
175g currants and sultanas mixed	

Rub the fats into the flour. Add the sugar and fruit. Add the salt and milk, mixing with a knife till it becomes a dough.

Place on a floured board and roll out 2 cm ($^3/_4$ in) thick. Score the top lightly with the back of a knife. Brush with milk, water or egg. Place on a flat baking tray: cook for 20 minutes at 400ºF (200ºC, gas mark 6). Cut into good size squares.

Proper heavy cake

An expert on Cornish cooking has told me that heavy cake should be 'shaley' on the top and have a 'heavy' line through the middle, and this might apply to the following recipe, though I have cheated a bit by using a little raising powder.

225g mixed fruit (three quarters currants, the rest sultanas)	
100g margarine	50g butter
400g plain flour	50g self-raising flour
a little peel (optional)	125g lard
75g sugar	$^1/_4$ teaspoon salt
300ml milk	

Place the flour in a bowl. Rub in the lard and margarine lightly; add the sugar, salt and fruit. Mix with the milk. Roll out the mixture on a floured board. Dab butter on two-thirds of the surface; fold the unbuttered side over and fold again. Rest for 30 minutes. Roll out again and fold in three. Rest a little then roll out 2cm ($^3/_4$ in) thick into a large round or square. Score criss-cross lines on top. Egg or milk wash. Bake at 400ºF (200ºC, gas mark 6) for about 20 minutes.

Some say heavy cake got its name from 'Hevva!', the cry the huer (the look-out on the cliffs) would shout when tell-tale signs of a shoal of fish appeared on the sea. It was the signal for the seiners to put to sea. Heavy cake is very popular in all the West Cornwall fishing ports and it is never baked without the netlike pattern on top.

Sweet buns

175g self-raising flour	125g margarine
150g castor sugar	50g mixed fruit
2 eggs	

Cream the margarine and sugar till white and fluffy. Add the eggs; stir in the flour and fruit gently. Spoon into greased bun tins or paper cases and bake in an oven at 350º-400ºF (180º-200ºC, gas mark 4-6) for 10 to 15 minutes.

You can omit the fruit and fill the bun when cool with jam and clotted cream.

Congress tarts
(Mrs Dale, Chyvarloe)

shortcrust pastry (or flaky if preferred)

125g ground almonds	jam
125g icing sugar	125g castor sugar
75g ground rice	1 large egg
1 egg white	

Prepare an almond filling by sieving the sugars, ground almonds and rice, and mixing with the egg.

Line bun tins with pastry and put some jam in the centre. Fill the case with a good teaspoon of the almond filling. Put a cross of pastry on the top and bake in the middle of the oven at 350ºF (180ºC, gas mark 4) for about half an hour. When they are pale brown on the bottom, they should be cooked.

Coconut haystacks

small tin condensed milk	225g desiccated coconut

Mix together and, to make haystacks, press small amounts of the mixture into a lightly greased egg cup. Shake out carefully onto greased baking sheet. Bake at 300-350ºF (150-180ºC, gas mark 2-4) for about 15 minutes until very light brown.

Coconut haystacks

(Mrs Nancy English, Porthleven)

225g desiccated coconut · 125g sugar

1 egg

Mix together and press small amounts into an egg cup or mould. Shake out onto a baking tray, and cook in a very moderate oven for twenty minutes or so till lightly browned.

Ginger biscuits

100g self-raising flour · 50g lard and butter mixed

2 tablespoons golden syrup · 1 level teaspoon cinnamon

2 level teaspoons ginger

1 level dessertspoon granulated sugar

$1/2$ teaspoon bicarbonate of soda

Sieve the dry ingredients. Melt the fats and syrup, then cool them and mix all the ingredients together. Break off pieces about the size of a walnut and place, well spaced, on a lightly greased baking tray. Bake for 15 minutes at 375ºF (190ºC, gas mark 5).

Chocolate cake

2 level teaspoons coffee powder (optional)

1 level teaspoon bicarbonate of soda

200g flour · 4 level tablespoons cocoa

2-3 teaspoons lemon juice · 180ml milk

175g castor sugar · 125g butter

2 eggs, beaten

Sieve the cocoa, flour and coffee powder together three times. Beat the butter and sugar together till light. Beat in eggs. Put the lemon juice into the milk, then add the bicarbonate of soda. Fold in the flour, etc together with the milk mixture. Put into a greased bread tin (the size for a large loaf) if you are making a cake, or in a Swiss roll tin for a gateau. For a cake, bake at 375ºF (190ºC, gas mark 5) for 40-60 minutes, testing with a skewer at 40 minutes. A gateau will need slightly less time. When cool, ice the cake with your favourite icing, or try 100g plain chocolate, 1 tablespoonful of rum and 25g butter, gently melted together.

For a gateau, turn out the chocolate sponge on to a wire tray. When almost cool, coat the top with 225g plain chocolate melted with 2 tablespoons of milk. When cold and firm, turn the cake over: spread the surface with some jam or raspberries, and then whipped double cream. Grate some chocolate on top. This cake improves with keeping.

Mrs Champion's Christmas cake

One Christmas we were staying at Gunwalloe and Mrs Champion invited us to tea. They had a lovely old farm kitchen and my brother and I were put to sit in the window seat, our feet barely touching the floor. On the table was the most magnificent fruit cake I had ever seen. It was plainly iced with something red stuck in the middle, but between the icing and the cake was a good 5cm (2 in) of marzipan.

By now I should think that anyone reading this will have realised that I was a child who loved her tummy. I cannot remember what else we had for tea that day. I know the table groaned, and that 'that' cake has stayed in my mind ever since.

Here are a few more recipes from the booklet from 1939, including Mrs Champion's cake.

Holly and robin cake
(Mrs E Champion, Chinalls, Gunwalloe)

1 lb (450g) self-raising flour and a good pinch of salt

12 oz (340g) butter	12 oz (340g) castor sugar
1 lb (450g) sultanas	4 oz (115g) candied peel
2 oz (50g) sweet almonds	4 oz (115g) glace cherries
1 tablespoon treacle	5 fresh eggs
1 tablespoon brandy	1 teaspoon mixed spice
a pinch of nutmeg	grated rind of half a lemon
juice of a small lemon	

1 dessertspoon caramel if a very dark cake is required

Prepare the fruit, shred and peel; cut cherries into quarters. Skin and chop the almonds, grate the lemon rind and add to the sieved flour with the salt and spices. Cream the butter and sugar, beating well together until thoroughly blended. Beat each egg separately with a tablespoon of flour. Stir in the dry ingredients, then the lemon juice, adding a little milk if necessary. Stir in the treacle, sufficient caramel to darken the cake, then the brandy. Pour the mixture into a prepared tin and scoop the centre of the cake towards the edges, making these higher so that the cake will bake level.

Bake in a moderate oven (Regulo mark 4) for $1^1/_2$ hours, then reduce to Mark 1. Allow from four to five hours.

When cold, wrap the cake in greaseproof paper and store.

Genoa cake
(Mrs M Freeman, Tregadjack, Mawgan)

10 oz (275g) flour	1/2 lb (225g) castor sugar
1 lb (450g) currants	4 oz (115g) almonds
1 teaspoon baking powder	1/2 lb (225g) butter
1/4 lb (115g) sultanas	10 oz (275g) candied peel
grated rind of lemon	3 eggs

Blanch the almonds and cut them in pieces. Wash the currants and clean the sultanas, beat the sugar and butter until light and creamy, add the flour, beat in the eggs and add the fruit and baking powder. Paper a shallow tin, pour in mixture and bake in a moderate oven from 1 to 1 1/2 hours. When cooked, brush top with white of egg and strew with chopped almonds.

Note: This would be an excellent tray-bake. Omit nuts; when cooked and cooled, cover with a thin layer of marzipan and then lemon icing.

Home-made toffee
(Miss Susan Joan Howe, Gunwalloe)

1/4 lb (115g) butter	3/4 lb (340g) brown sugar
6 oz (175g) syrup	1 teaspoon lemon juice
1 teaspoon water	

Melt the ingredients, bring to the boil slowly and continue boiling for 15 minutes – stirring all the time. Test whether sufficiently cooked by placing a teaspoonful of toffee in a cup of cold water, when it should set quite firmly.

Now pour molten toffee into buttered tins and, when cold, break into pieces.

Grandmother's cake
(Mrs Stewart Lugg, Toll, Gunwalloe)

1 rounded teaspoon bicarbonate of soda

1 cup (225g) brown sugar	3 1/2 cups (400g) flour
1 level tablespoon cinnamon	[too much, in my opinion! H.M.]
1 cup thick sour cream	1 lb (450g) stoned raisins
1/2 cup treacle	

Measure with large (1/2 pt, 280ml) teacup. Pour the slightly warmed treacle into the mixing bowl, add the soda dissolved in a little warm water, then work in the flour, sugar and cream. Beat well, add cinnamon and raisins. Bake in a moderate oven for one hour.

Walnut gingerbread
(Mrs Owen Lugg)

3 cups flour	$1/2$ cup milk
1 teaspoon bircarb.	$1/2$ cup butter
1 cup Lyle's golden syrup	$1/2$ cup sugar
1 teaspoon ground ginger	1 cup chopped walnuts
pinch of salt	

Beat the butter and sugar, Stir in the ginger and syrup. Dissolve the bicarbonate of soda in milk, add to the mixture with sifted flour, salt and walnuts. Pour into a greased shallow tin (a roasting dish). Bake in a moderate oven for one hour.

FRUIT

Fruit was usually bought for special occasions. An orange each in the Christmas stocking was an annual treat. Quite often, Gran Gilbert, who liked oranges, would buy a couple of Jaffas, large and juicy. Grandad, who had been to Africa steamboating, insisted the orange was peeled the right way so that the pith came off cleanly. The orange would then be divided into 'pasties' and shared around. Gran saved the peel to simmer gently with sugar and a little water till it candied, and carefully smoothed out the large coloured square of tissue paper that the orange had been wrapped in, for her use and mine! Lemons too were beautifully wrapped. Lemons were for pancakes and drinks, cold in summer and hot in winter.

Grandad was very young when he went round the world. He brought back stalks of bananas and exciting bits and pieces like calabashes for his young family.

Grapes were bought, as they are now, for anyone ill. Strawberries were a treat at St Peterstide. We picked loads of blackberries in season and there were windfalls from the apple trees at Content, where Uncle Fred also had many gooseberry, blackcurrant, raspberry and loganberry bushes. Rhubarb was grown by Uncle George, who had an allotment, and by Uncle Charlie, both keen gardeners.

Dried fruits, apricots, figs and especially prunes, were very popular. Tinned pears or peaches might be bought for a special treat for Sunday tea-time, but usually it was jelly and custard or blancmange and prunes, 'which are good for you'.

SUPPER OR LATE TEA

For this something savoury was preferred. Salted cod or fresh fish, fried or scrowled over the fire, tripe and onions, hog's pudding from the butcher or liver fried with onions, ham from a knuckle, marinated pilchards or fish and chips from Tregembo's where 'Harry' would cook pollack specially for Gran. A piece of leftover pasty would fill a gap or tasty sausages from James' shop in Helston. Sausages and 'scrowls' (pork scratchings) could be bought too, from Mrs Eddy's house in the little island beside Fore Street Chapel.

I can just remember visiting Mrs Eddy with Gran: the long crowded old room was darkened by the masses of leaves and bushes outside her far window and beside Mrs Eddy was her parrot, of whom I was terrified. Mrs Eddy was a character and surely harmless, but I hung on to Gran's long black skirts – petrified.

Hog's pudding is a kind of 'white' black pudding, and recipes are closely guarded, but this sausage recipe is very good.

Sausages

450g bread (stale)	1.5 kg lean pork
450g fat pork (not flare)	25g salt
$1^1/_2$ level teasp. ground mace	$^1/_2$ level teasp. ground ginger
$^1/_4$ level teasp. ground or chopped sage	
some flour	900ml cold water

Soak the bread in 900ml cold water. Put the pork through a coarse mincer. Add salt and seasonings. Mix well. Squeeze water from the bread amd mix it with the meat mixture. Replace the mincer with a small cutter and put the mixture through again. Test for salt by frying a little sausage in a pan, adjusting seasoning if necessary. Shape into sausages with flour. Cook for 20 minutes or so.

Marinated pilchards

Take a dozen or so pilchards. Gut, scrape off the scales and behead them but leave in the bones. Wash and lay them in a pie dish, sprinkle with a few whole pickling spices, a little salt, pepper and sugar to taste, and cover with a mixture of three parts malt vinegar to one part water, laying bay leaves along the top. Cover with greaseproof paper and then with a piece of brown paper, tucking the paper around the dish edge to seal. Put into a hot oven till bubbling, then turn down the heat to 200^{0}F (90-100^{0}C) or less (the lowest gas mark you have) and cook gently for at least twelve hours. Eat cold. Spiced vinegar may be used instead of malt vinegar and spices.

DRINKS

There was tea to drink for the grown-ups and cocoa for the children. Coffee was almost unknown except for Camp coffee with chicory.

Gran Gilbert made real lemonade. If she thought we needed 'building up' she would make an egg nog (egg whisked into hot milk with nutmeg) or else liver salts to clean out our insides. These salts were just like the commercial ones, but no one in the family can remember the recipe. There was no escape from Syrup of Figs, a weekly dose.

Alcohol was rarely bought. Uncle George made gallons of non-alcoholic 'herby beer', which is very refreshing. Herby beer can be made by buying a bottle of herb beer mixture from a good chemist and following the instructions.

At Content, Aunt Hettie made blackberry wine. This was surprising as she was strictly tee-total. Aunt Hettie lived with her in-laws and I think she made wine after her father-in-law died. He was a dear old man, staunchly methodist and a local preacher.

It was a tied cottage, but once it had been a holding in its own right. The kitchen with its bare red flagged tiles worn with age reminded

me of my favourite book, *Lorna Doone*. The room was large and looked sparsely furnished but it had a long wooden scrubbed table in front of the window, a big carver for Uncle Fred to sit in (after his father died), a large armchair, lots of small chairs and another table with plants on. A large china dresser stood against a wall which was partitioned off from a back room. Built into the old fireplace were cupboards each side of a Cornish range. Kindling wood was kept in these, whole long branches in one, the day's supply in the other. They were usually apple branches. The lichen fell off in great pieces and insects and gramma sows (woodlice) crawled everywhere. Aunt Hettie swept them up with a witch's broom. The fireplace extended through to the other side of the wall and there you could walk into an enormous chimney and look up at the sky.

About a hundred years ago the gardens around the house had been well laid out. A lemon tree leaned against the house and roses climbed around the corner and over the outside closet. All the way on up to the orchard were hydrangea, rose and fruit bushes, all tangled up. In front of the house a small lawn tried hard to survive. Here Aunt Hettie reared her baby chicks in coops where she could keep her eye on them and they had some protection from owls, foxes and buzzards.

Beyond was another copse surrounded by tall trees. It was a wonderful secret place for us children. Pampas bushes and pittosporam towered over us and brambles held us captive. It was cool and dark, the foliage letting in little shafts of sunlight here and there. I was puzzled by the number of shiny brown bottles lying everywhere. When you trod on them they didn't break but sank into the soft mulch of pine needles, small branches and rotting leaves.

Years later Aunt Hettie told me that Uncle Fred used to bring home a couple of bottles of beer for his mother when he went to town on his motorbike. Mrs Reed smuggled them upstairs to drink and would not be seen bringing them down empty so she used to fling them from her bedroom window across the little grass patch, sometimes hitting the beautiful laburnum tree in the centre. Mrs Reed was born at Helford, and was, I suspect, Church of England.

There was and probably still is a great divide between chapel and church, but the fact is that before the Wesleys visited Cornwall there were several 'kiddlywinks' in every Cornish village, however small.

Some of the old Cornish drinks sound lethal, but certainly warming. Samson was cider and rum boiled together with honey. Chenagrum

was hot beer, rum, sliced lemon, nutmeg and sugar. 'Christmas drink' consisted of two lumps of sugar, a wineglass of rum, lemon and hot water. 'Mahogany' was two parts gin to one part treacle.

Cornish punch was made with half a bottle of cognac, a tumbler of lemon juice, 2-4 lb (1-2kg) cane sugar; all put into a gallon container and filled up with boiling water.

Grandad Bray had a good supply of red wine. At some date in the thirties kegs of wine had washed in on the shore from Fishing Cove to Praa Sands. I have been told that they were pipes (over two metres tall) and that it was raw claret, not yet matured. This wine lasted years and a bottle at a time was kept in the little bible cupboard beside the fireplace in Grandad's sitting room. Occasionally my brother and I would be allowed to have some. A quarter tumbler of red wine, a large spoonful of sugar, and the glass topped up with hot water. We didn't tell Gran at Porthleven.

One evening Father and Mother went from Porthleven to Gunwalloe to fetch some of the wine. It's a long walk across the cliffs, separated halfway by a good ten minutes' trudge on shingle – the Loe Bar.

On the way back, after crossing the Bar, they sat, emptied their shoes of pebbles and rested a while. They were getting anxious about the time when they saw a man approaching, pushing his bike across the stretch towards them. It was now dusk and they stood up to make enquiries. Father was six feet tall; Mother tall also, thin as a wraith. These two figures suddenly rising out of the ground in the mist, bottles clinking in the frail they were carrying, was too much for the poor man. He turned tail, bike and all, and was swallowed up in the darkness. In vain Father shouted to reassure him, 'It's only me, Percy Gilbert.' They never found out who he was. In those days the Loe Bar route from Gunwalloe or Mullion was a short cut, saving miles around Helston for people who lived at Breage and Ashton as well as Porthleven.

Porthleven had few 'gentry'. The Squire, a couple of miles away in his manor at Penrose, was distant and his great authority did not affect the fishermen, who did not depend on his goodwill for work or housing. There was the vicar, 'well educated', liked and tolerated, though Pap did not approve of him dressing in a 'frock'. The Methodist ministers were respected, but in their place. The chapels were firmly run by stewards. As for Doctor Elliston, for whom Mother cooked, his word was gospel and his advice is quoted still.

Doctor Elliston's wife was a genteel woman, very generous with her food. 'Doctor', a large boisterous man, liked a good table. They had one daughter, Hope. When the family had finished their dinner, the servants were welcome to cut as much meat off the joint as they wished for their own meal. This was unusual then, and would be more than generous today. Mother, Bella and Trissie tucked in, in true Cornish style.

Mrs Elliston also permitted Mother to take home any poultry carcasses for Granny Gilbert. This was a great treat as the bones were quite well covered. Gran would pick off all the meat and make broth with the bones. Once when Gran Gilbert was ill, Mrs Elliston sent down a huge two pint moulded Russian cream. It sat on a plate on the washstand by Gran's bedside, firm as a rock with three clear layers. I know now that it must have had more gelatine in it than Mother's, whose Russian cream when turned out slowly subsided and was a lovely light texture. I know I eyed that Russian cream, but I cannot remember eating any of it. Ill or not, probably Gran ate the lot.

Mother made ice-cream. Grandad Gilbert fetched dry ice from Pawlyn's to freeze the custard and we all helped with turning the handle of the wooden tub it was made in. At Christmas she made about a dozen cakes. Some were three colour sponges with soft butter fillings, others walnut, covered with American icing, which I have never mastered as well. There were saffron cakes and rich fruit ones which Mother would struggle to ice. We are lucky today with ingredients all ready and easy to use.

Puddings and cakes took a day to prepare. Currants had to be thoroughly washed, spread out on paper and put in a rack overnight to dry. Raisins needed stoning, a lovely sticky job, and sultanas were put in a large sieve and two or three lots of flour shaken through them till the flour came out clean. Almonds were blanched and chopped, and the butter and sugar had a beat from two or three of us to get it soft and fluffy. When the cake was made, Mother would open the oven door and feel the heat before putting the cake in and wait anxiously till it was safely out of the oven without burning – there was no thermostat on a slab!

I think the hardest job of all was icing the cakes. Was all icing sugar

as lumpy as Mum's? I can hear the crunch now as she rolled and rolled the lumps out. Then she shook the sugar through a fine sieve. She wrote Merry Christmas beautifully on each cake, but sometimes a piece of sugar would stick in the nozzle and the whole lot would have to be put back in the bowl and the icing gun washed out in hot water. Father would fuss at all this activity for neighbours and relations, but it made no difference: Christmas wouldn't have been the same without all that cooking.

Mother's nearest neighbours were Mr and Mrs Peter Williams whose house was built slightly lower than ours. Wooden steps placed along the wall saved walking down our path and up theirs. The Williams' kitchen was almost as familiar as our own. The room was rather dark because a glass-roofed outer room had been built on, but the light seemed to shine onto a picture of an old man kneeling on a form in a plain chapel. He was praying and it seemed to bless the kitchen table immediately below the picture. I thought the old man looked like Willie Allen who sat in the middle of the chapel on Sundays. He sold fish all week, but on Sundays he looked different in his best suit; his bald head, hatless once a week, shone like a dollar. We sat above in the gallery in our family seat and for the morning service we were free of grown-ups. My cousins André and Jack flicked rolled up sweet papers at Mr Allen's head. He never batted an eyelid even when they scored a direct hit. In the front seat opposite Margaret Jane Toy, father's cousin, frowned at all of us.

The slab in Mrs Williams' kitchen was in the far corner where Tiny the dog slept for most of the day in a chair beside it. A door with a tiny knob hid a narrow stair which led to the back rooms where the three boys slept.

Mr and Mrs Williams had a business at the foot of Salt Cellar Hill on the quay and mother often lit their slab during the late afternoon. It was a cantankerous old thing and she sometimes doused it with paraffin to get it going. One day she poured a good drop over and when she threw in the lighted match there was an almighty bang and the dog was shot from one end of the room to the other. Hugh, one of the boys, had left petrol in the can. After that the dog always ran away when he saw Mother coming.

I was envious of the boys. They wore huge aprons for their Sunday meals. This seemed a good idea to me: I had to change. As soon as I got in from chapel I had to go upstairs, take off my Sunday dress, put on another, then change again for Sunday School and go through the same performance later for tea. The truth is, I could not be trusted with a pinny; summer best was that awful crêpe-de-chine which was murder to wash.

Food has changed quite a bit everywhere during the past few decades. Most of us now eat salads and plenty of fruit. The farmers' wives no longer cook large joints of 'tag' or 'boxheater' for harvest dinners – combine harvesters have done away with the need for a dozen or so men working in the field shocking up the corn, or helping on threshing day with the old steam thresher, which went from farm to farm at the end of summer.

No one seems to have the time to spend in the kitchen, cooking the quantities our mothers and grandmothers did. We can only look back and marvel at their good tempers in the face of baking, washing and ironing all around the slab, and coping with its 'smeach' when it smoked. It had to be riddled, lit, tended, coached and cleaned every day till it shone black. There it was, the centre of our lives, brass handles shining, cooking dinners and baking in its oven. It kept the kettle hot and clothes on the boil; there was room to heat the iron, scald cream and dry off kindling wood, all on the surface. The rack provided the right warmth to rise the yeast and air clean clothes. New baby chicks could be nursed in the fender and wet shoes and boots dried overnight.

Will our children and grandchildren have the same regard for the electric or gas cooker? for fish fingers and baked beans? for Milky Bars instead of jam paste to fill up a gap on the way home from school?

I feel I was lucky. I lived half my childhood with Gran and Grandad. The village was a close-knit community and we knew everyone. It was full of aunts, uncles and cousins, and I traipsed around with Gran to them all, from Auntie Violet's cocoa to sweet buns from Auntie Annie, heavy cake at Aunt Hartie's. Wonderful holidays all months of the year at Content.

We lived and worked in an environment that had not changed for a long time. The legacy those days left is rich and I hope it will not disappear completely.